Books are

Costume in Context
The Tudors

Jennifer Ruby

B.T. Batsford Ltd, London

Foreword

When studying costume it is important to understand the difference between fashion and costume. Fashion tends to predict the future – that is, what people *will* be wearing – and very fashionable clothes are usually worn only by people wealthy enough to afford them. For example, even today, the clothes that appear in fashionable magazines are not the same as those being worn by the majority of people in the street. Costume, on the other hand, represents what people are actually wearing at a given time, which may be quite different from what is termed 'fashionable' for their day.

Each book in this series is built round a fictitious family. By following the various members, sometimes over several generations – and the people with whom they come into contact – you will be able to see the major fashion developments of the period and compare the clothing and lifestyles of people from all walks of life. You will meet servants, soldiers, street-sellers and beggars as well as the very wealthy, and you will see how their different clothing reflects their particular occupations and circumstances.

Major social changes are mentioned in each period and you will see how clothing is adapted as people's needs and attitudes change. The date list will help you to understand more fully how historical events affect the clothes that people wear.

Many of the drawings in these books has been taken from contemporary paintings. During the course of your work perhaps you could visit some museums and art galleries yourself in order to learn more about the costumes of the period you are studying from the artists who painted at that time.

Acknowledgments

The sources for the drawings in this book have, in some cases, been sixteenth-century paintings. In particular: pages 3, 18, 19, 28 and 29 after Hans Holbein the Younger; pages 23, 25 and 27 after Pieter Bruegel; and page 35 after Hieronymous Bosch. In the colour section: Henry VIII after Hans Holbein the Younger, Sir Martin Frobisher after Cornelius Ketel, 'The Bagpiper' after Albrecht Durer, Queen Elizabeth I after Marcus Gheeraets the Younger and 'Young Man' after I. Oliver.

© Jennifer Ruby 1987
First published 1987
Reprinted 1993

Typeset by Tek-Art Ltd, Kent
and printed in Great Britain by
The Bath Press, Avon
for the publishers
B.T. Batsford Ltd
4 Fitzhardinge Street
London W1H 0AH

ISBN 0 7134 5471 7

Contents

lady-in-waiting
(c. 1520)

Date List

1485	End of the Wars of the Roses. Henry VII comes to the throne. The beginning of a period of greater stability in Britain.
1509	Henry VIII comes to the throne. Male fashion takes on a square, masculine look. Women's clothes have simple, flowing lines.
1520	The Field of Cloth of Gold. Henry VIII meets the French King in France and demonstrates his power with a magnificent display of gorgeous clothing.
1532	Henry marries Anne Boleyn. Anne has spent some time in France and likes some of the French fashions. These are copied in England.
1533	The beginnings of the dissolution of the monasteries, which leaves many monks homeless and many more with nowhere to go for shelter when in trouble.
1536	Rebellion against enclosure of common land, which has caused great hardship to many already poor people.
1547	Henry VIII succeeded by Edward VI. There is little change in fashion during Edward's reign as the King is too young to take a great interest in clothes.
1553	Mary Tudor becomes Queen.
1554	Mary marries Philip of Spain. This marks the beginning of Spanish influence on English fashions. Introduction of the ruff and Spanish farthingale.
1558	Mary succeeded by her sister Elizabeth. Female fashion gradually becomes squarer and more masculine. Men's clothes take on a more feminine appearance, with small waists and exaggerated hips.
1564	Starch is introduced into England by a Dutch lady. She gives lessons in starching to wealthy ladies, enabling the ruff to become very exaggerated.
1569	Second rebellion aginst enclosures.
1570-3	Francis Drake carries out raiding expeditions to Spain and brings back many treasures to England.
1572	First Poor Law introduced, aimed at relieving the destitute poor.
1577-80	Drake becomes the first English mariner to sail around the world. The 'peascod' belly becomes popular for men, exaggerating the stomach.
1588	The Spanish Armada.
1600	The East India Company is formed. The increased trade means that many spices, pomanders, silks, satins, velvets and lace are imported and used in the making of fashionable garments.
1603	The death of Queen Elizabeth and the end of the Tudor dynasty. James VI of Scotland becomes James I of England, the first Stuart monarch.

Introduction

In Tudor times life was very different from what we know today. There were no vast housing estates, factories, cars, aeroplanes or machines, but miles of untouched and uninhabited countryside, interspersed with small towns and tiny villages. There were no telephones, televisions or sophisticated postal services, but messengers who rode for days on horseback. People tended not to travel far and communication was a slow process. Those living in outlying districts simply did not know what was taking place at Court and in Parliament. A new fashion in clothing, for example, could take from five to 15 years to travel from London to other areas of the country.

Fashions tended to originate at Court and were often influenced by the foreign policy of the time. At the beginning of the sixteenth century there was a strong German influence on northern European fashions. This meant that many bright colours were used and slashing was a favourite form of decoration. The most common materials were velvet, satin and cloth of gold, and red was a popular colour – although this was worn only by the nobility. Suddenly, in the middle of the century, everything changed, and the colourful and flamboyant clothes of earlier years gave way to Spanish fashions, which were more tightly fitted and often black. In 1554, Mary Tudor married King Philip of Spain and we can see the Spanish influence beginning at about this time. It continued throughout the century, even when England and Spain were at war. The ruff, the farthingale, bombasting (padding), and the tiny waists for men and women which dominated fashions in the second half of the century gave a stiff, rigid and proud appearance to the wearers, in contrast to the more flowing lines that had gone before.

The reign of Elizabeth I was a time of adventures and discoveries and these also had their effect on fashion. Drake and Raleigh's expeditions to South America and the New World, and Sir John Mildenhall's to India to form the East India Trading Company, resulted in England becoming richer from captured treasure and increased trade overseas. With these discoveries came spices, pomanders, pearls and new and beautiful fabrics; silks, satins, velvets, lace and calico arrived from abroad, and wool, which was a major national product, was exported.

While all these beautiful things were worn by the rich, however, the dress of the poorer people changed very little. The beautiful fabrics, ornaments, wiring and supports worn by the wealthy would, in any case, have been out of place for working people, who needed to be practical as well as thrifty. Simple garments of coarse linen or English wool would, therefore, have been most usual for them.

nobleman
(c. 1565)

5

tradesman's
wife (c. 1540)

water carrier
(c. 1520)

shepherd
(c. 1570)

working girl
(c. 1563)

sailor
(c. 1598)

6

In between the nobility and the poor were the middle classes. These were people like merchants, doctors and lawyers who were respected and often considerably wealthy. Their costume would frequently denote their profession. For example, a scholar would usually be seen in a flat cap and gown. Merchants could often afford better and more costly fabrics than some of the nobility, but they did not have the same social standing. Consequently, they sometimes tried to marry their children into the aristocracy in order to obtain a better social status. This often worked, as titled families frequently needed the merchants' money!

You will find many of these people represented in this book and perhaps you would like to think about some of these points whilst you are reading it. Ask yourself if their clothes are practical for their particular lifestyle, and think about how their style of dress reflects their position in society. You could also look at some of the historical events of the period and see how these affected the shape and type of clothes in Tudor times.

fashionable ladies (c. 1580)

falconer (c. 1875)

A Nobleman, c. 1500

On the right you can see a young nobleman at the court of Henry VII. He is dressed in the latest fashionable style.

He wears a tight-fitting doublet which is short, reaching only to this waist. It has very full sleeves, gathered into the wrist and slashed from the wrist to the elbow. There are also slashes on the front of the doublet which have been symmetrically arranged. 'Slashing' was very popular at this time and simply meant to cut slits of varying length into a garment. The undershirt or lining was then pulled through these slits to form decorative pouches. The young man's shirt is made of holland, which is a type of linen. It has a fairly low neckline which tends to emphasize his shoulders, giving him a very strong, masculine appearance.

His hose are tight and are fastened to his doublet with points. Points were ties which fastened through eyelet holes on the hose and corresponding eyelet holes on the doublet. The codpiece – a simple covering used when men wore hose – is one of the earliest types and is also fastened with points. The short loose stockings over the hose are made of silk and the very wide shoes are made of velvet. His beautiful gown is edged with fur and is richly embroidered. Short gowns coming down to the knee like this one were generally preferred by young men. The nobleman's hair is long, and he wears a small, soft-crowned hat with a turned up brim fastened with a brooch.

Below you can see an example of points and how they worked. They are like laces, fastening the doublet to the hose. On the ends of the points were metal tags or 'aiglets'. The aiglets of rich people like this nobleman were often precious metal or jewels. You will notice also that there is a seam in the back of the hose. A nobleman like this would be very anxious to get his seams straight when he was getting dressed so that he looked perfectly turned out when he was finally ready.

Below, on the left, is another of the nobleman's hats. This one is also made of velvet, is small and round but does not have a front brim.

The nobleman usually carries a leather pouch suspended from his belt when he goes out. One of them is pictured here.

Finally, you can see in more detail a sleeve of another of his many doublets. This sleeve is made in two parts which are fastened together with points. The sleeve has been slashed. You can imagine that it was essential for a nobleman such as this to have a valet to help him get dressed. What a time it must have taken!

silver engraved ring

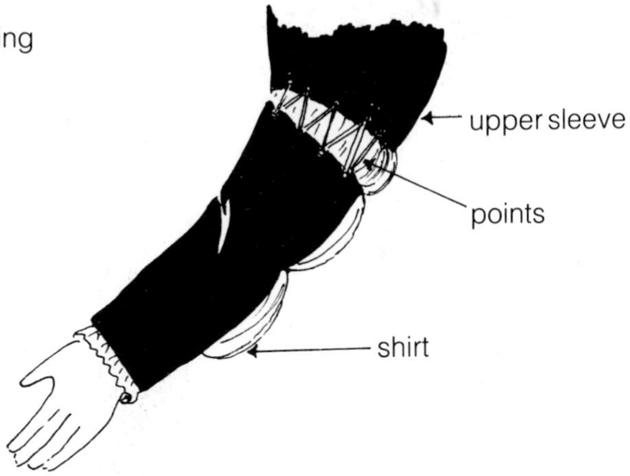

upper sleeve

points

shirt

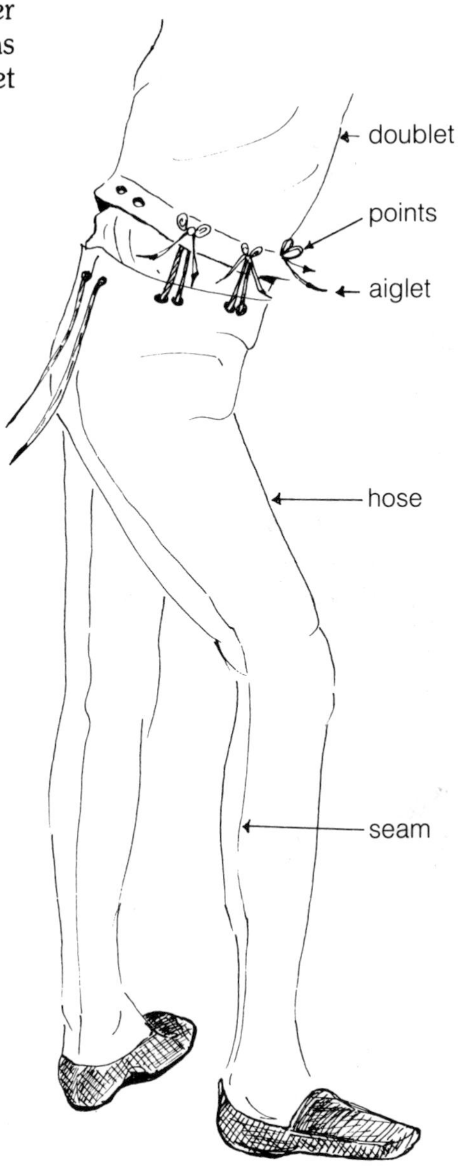

doublet

points

aiglet

hose

seam

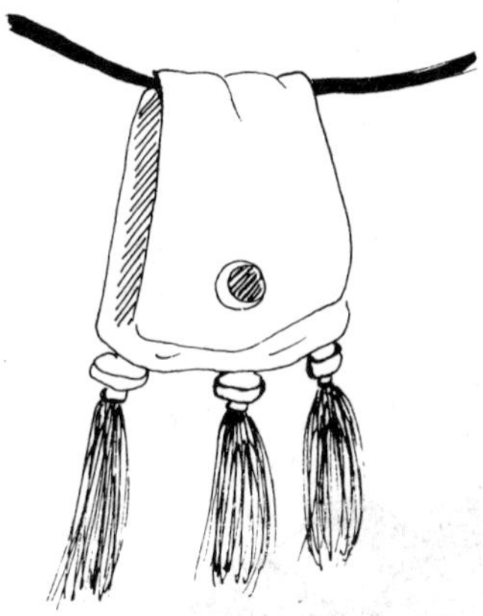

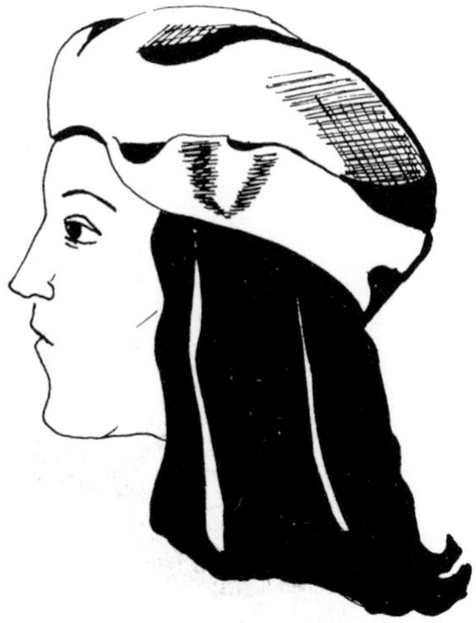

A Lady-in-Waiting, c. 1500

This young girl of 14 is a lady-in-waiting to Elizabeth of York, King Henry VII's queen. She is betrothed to the nobleman on the previous page. When they are married they will live in his family's castle in the Midlands.

She is wearing a gown of heavy green satin, lined with velvet. This rich lining is displayed both on the sleeves of the garment, which are turned back, and at the rear, as the long, full train has been fastened up to the waistband with a brooch. The bodice of the gown is tight-fitting and has a square neckline, the opening of which has been partly filled with dark velvet.

Her hood has a full hanging piece at the back and a coloured lining turned back from the face. You can see that the sides of the hood are split part way up and she wears the front pieces over her shoulders as is the fashion.

train fastened with brooch

Another of the lady-in-waiting's hoods is pictured on the right. It is called a 'gable' hood because of the distinctive shape of the front, which is maintained by wires or a stiffened framework. It is beautifully decorated, as you can see. Her hair is parted in the middle and she also wears an undercap of linen under the hood. The gable hood became very popular and was worn for many years. In fact, even today, if you look at a pack of cards you will see the queen is usually portrayed in this distinctive head gear.

Underneath her gown and over a linen chemise (like the male shirt), it is usual for her to wear a kirtle. This is a simple frock with a tight-fitting bodice and sleeves and a full skirt. It is usually hidden by the gown. However, sometimes, she might wear the kirtle on its own, as it appears in the picture on the bottom right. In this case, she would probably choose to decorate it with a girdle and perhaps a purse and some beads.

All these layers of clothing might appear excessive to us, but we must remember that in Tudor times there were no small, centrally heated living rooms and these people needed many clothes to keep them warm in the vast and draughty halls and galleries at Court.

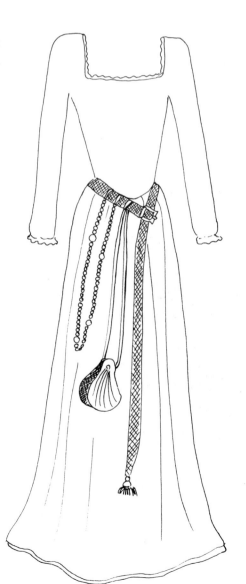

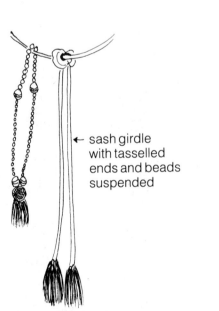

← sash girdle with tasselled ends and beads suspended

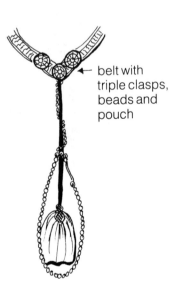

← belt with triple clasps, beads and pouch

The Nobleman in Later Life, c. 1530

It is now 1530 and the nobleman and his wife are living in the Midlands with their family and servants. You can see how the fashions have changed.

The nobleman is wearing a doublet which is highly decorated with slashings and embroidery. On top of this he has a sleeveless jerkin, similar in style to the one pictured on the opposite page, and, over this, a velvet gown edged with fur. You will notice that the short sleeves of the gown have also been slashed and the white satin lining has been drawn through for decoration.

With his flat cap and wide shoes, you can see that the overall look is a broad, square one, with the emphasis on the wide, masculine shoulders.

One of the most noticeable differences between this costume and the earlier one is the change that has taken place in the hose, which now has two distinct parts: the upper stocks, or breeches, and the nether stocks, or lower half. The upper stocks were often made of a different material to the nether stocks and were slashed and decorated like those in the picture opposite, giving the appearance of a pair of shorts. The codpiece was now worn much larger and was often highly decorated and padded. Some men even used them as pincushions!

Shoes were becoming extremely wide at this time. In fact, Henry VIII passed a law during his reign limiting the width of shoes to six inches! You can see some of the nobleman's shoes pictured here.

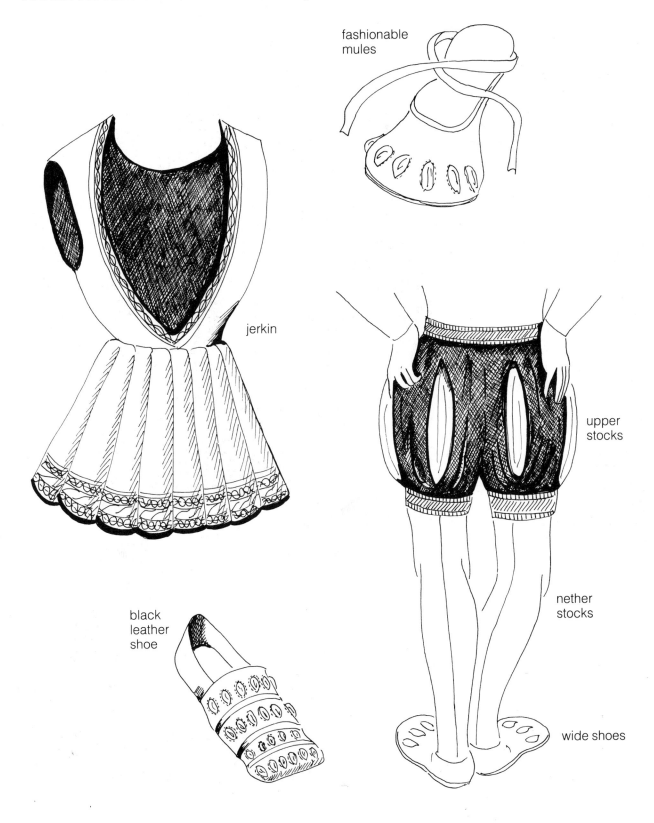

fashionable mules

jerkin

upper stocks

nether stocks

black leather shoe

wide shoes

Here is the nobleman's wife. She is wearing a trained kirtle which has a fitted bodice. She has decorated the low, square neck with pearls. The sleeves of the kirtle have immense fur cuffs and her undersleeves are slashed along the back seam revealing her chemise underneath. On her head she is wearing a gable hood with the side pieces (called 'lappets') turned up, leaving the sides of her linen undercap showing below. Around her waist she is wearing a jewelled girdle.

Some of her gowns are made of deep crimson and blue velvet, which are colours that, by law, only nobility can wear. The long train of her gowns and kirtles also indicates rank or wealth. In fact, very often throughout history, a lot of material symbolized a lot of money!

Here are some more items from the noblewoman's wardrobe. Her shoes, like her husband's, are wide and are often padded and slashed for decoration. You can also see how she wears her hair under her cap and hood.

The deep, rich colours and beautiful decorations on these clothes cannot be over-emphasized, yet, underneath this fine adornment, women were, by our standards, very dirty. People did not bathe and fresh air was thought to be bad for the lungs. Many women used to carry a posy of flowers with them in order to disguise the bad smells that were around them. The men were just as bad, of course. Henry VIII used to carry an orange with him when he walked in the streets. The inside of the orange had been taken out and the skin filled with a sponge full of vinegar and spices. He used to smell this constantly to counteract the foul stench in the streets.

You might like to compare this with attitudes today. We wear simple clothes compared to the Tudors, but we pay much more attention to what is underneath our outer garments by taking time and trouble over personal hygiene. Which do you think is the most important, outward appearance or cleanliness? Why do you think this change in attitudes has occurred?

jewellery

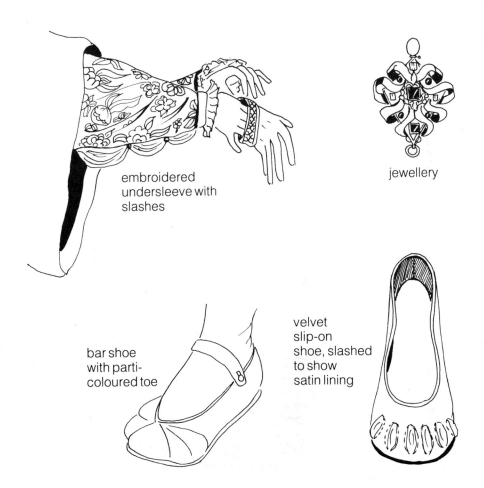

embroidered
undersleeve with
slashes

bar shoe
with parti-
coloured toe

velvet
slip-on
shoe, slashed
to show
satin lining

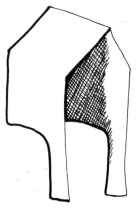

linen undercap

The Nobleman's Family, c. 1534

This is Lady Margaret, one of the nobleman's daughters. She is wearing a gable headdress with the side pieces turned up and the black tails hanging loose. Her hair is concealed in rolls. You will notice that she has a small posy of flowers at her neck. Like many ladies, she wears this to counteract all the bad smells in the air.

Her husband, Sir Thomas, is pictured on the right. He is wearing a flat cap and he has a beard and side whiskers, which were just becoming fashionable at this time.

Below, you can see Hannah, the nurse to their children. She has been with the family for some years and was Margaret's nurse when she was a child. She is wearing a flat cap over an undercap of linen.

One of Hannah's jobs is to look after the new baby, Elizabeth, who you can see on the opposite page. It was the custom that all children started life in swaddling clothes. The baby was dressed in a cotton or linen shirt and then bandaged tightly to include its arms and feet. It was thought that this tight bandaging would enable the child to grow straight, protect it from harm and make it easier to carry. The baby would also wear a 'biggin', a little cap.

c. 1534

Can you think of any harmful effects that this type of dress might have on such a tiny infant? Perhaps you could compare these ideas on caring for a new-born baby with our very different methods and attitudes today.

This is Richard, Margaret's two-year-old son. Children were always dressed as adults in Tudor times, and little boys were dressed as girls until they were about five or six. Richard is wearing a long gown with hanging sleeves. The gown is beautifully decorated with gold trimming. Under his flat cap he wears a coif, a linen cap which fits closely to his head and ties under his chin. His shoes have fashionably broad toes.

Once again, this costume appears very strange to us because it does not allow for the freedom of movement which a small boy like this would need and desire.

A Merchant and His Daughter, c. 1534

This is Mary, the 16-year-old daughter of a successful cloth merchant. Mary's father has conducted some business with the nobleman and, because of this, she has been given the opportunity to live in at the castle as a lady-in-waiting to the nobleman's wife.

She is wearing a gown with a low, square neck which has been filled in with a buttoned partlet made of lawn. The gown has ornamental shoulder bands and the sleeves have velvet cuffs which match the velvet strip down the front. The skirt is hitched up with clasps at the front, revealing her kirtle beneath. Around her waist she is wearing a sash girdle with beads suspended from it and, once again, her hair is entirely hidden by her hood.

Although Mary's clothes are quite fashionable, you will notice that they are not as richly decorated as those of her mistress.

On the right you can see her father, Henry Wyngate. He is sitting at his desk opening some correspondence. His writing tools look most unusual to us in these days of typewriters and sophisticated electronic equipment!

Henry is quite an affluent man due to his successful business enterprises. Consequently, he can afford rich clothing. Being a cloth merchant he can easily obtain fine silks, satins, velvets and brocades, which are then sent to his tailor and made up for him.

Over his shirt, which is quite high at the neck, he is wearing a doublet of satin and an embroidered jerkin. His gown is made of velvet, is lined and faced with fur and has short, full sleeves which are beautifully embroidered.

Henry is ambitious for himself and his children. Edmund, one of his sons, is also in the nobleman's employ as a herald, and Henry has hopes that Mary might marry into the nobleman's family.

Domestic Servants, c. 1534

The young people that you see working here are from the same family. Their father is a farmer on the nobleman's estate. John is working in the garden. In Tudor times many rich people took a great pride in their beautifully kept gardens, which were often arranged in complicated, geometric patterns. John's upbringing has given him a knowledge of plants and here he is tending the herbs. He is wearing a simple outfit consisting of a flat cap, a leather jerkin over a shirt, thick hose and a pair of loose boots which just cover his ankles.

His sister Ruth is cleaning the bedroom of one of the ladies-in-waiting. She is wearing a straight kirtle of coarse linen material with the sleeves rolled up, a bibless apron and a neckerchief around her shoulders. Although her hair is pinned up out of the way, she has no head covering, which is very unusual. Perhaps you might like to think of a reason why she is without any kind of hood when it was the custom for Tudor ladies to keep their head covered at all times.

Her sister Jane is in another part of the castle helping with the washing. She has her hair bound in a net and is wearing her kirtle hitched up to keep it out of the wet. She is beating the laundry to help to get rid of some of the water.

The work for these girls is hard and long, and as they have very little money they make their own clothes and then try to preserve them from damage as best they can.

Sometimes, as these lines from a contemporary poem tell us, girls like Ruth and Jane would even go without their shoes:

*She would go barefoot for to save
Her shoes and hose for they were dear . . .*
(Thomas Churchyard, *Churchyard Chippes*)

This costume is very different from the fine garments of the ladies we have seen so far. However, in spite of all this, the girls think themselves lucky to be employed by the nobleman as they will receive a good education in household affairs and, perhaps, if they are fortunate, occasionally cast-off clothes from the ladies-in-waiting.

A Farmer and His Wife, c. 1534

This is William, the father of the three servants you have just seen. He is doing quite well for himself as a farmer on the nobleman's estate. William, of course, has little time or interest in fashion, and his clothes are plain, sturdy and practical. He is wearing a soft hat and a canvas jerkin over a coarse linen shirt. He has overstockings on top of his hose, and his thick-

soled leather boots are fastened with a tab front. He carries a leather bag and a knife.

His wife, Alice, is at home in their cottage with their youngest child, Gilbert, who is two years old. She is spinning.

Alice is wearing a white linen hood and apron and a plain cotton gown with a kirtle beneath. The tails of her hood and the skirt of her gown are both pinned up out of the way whilst she is working. Her keys and purse are suspended from her waist.

Gilbert is wearing an old tunic of John's over a simple cotton dress and is barefoot. You might like to compare his garments with those of Richard on page 17. Which child, do you think, is the most comfortable?

A Farm Labourer and His Wife, c. 1534

When Alice looks out of her window she can see the fields and some of the farm labourers busy working on the harvest. This is Adam. He is tired from the long, heavy work in the August sunshine and has paused for a break. He is wearing only a shirt, hose and boots because it is so hot. As he has removed his doublet you can quite clearly see the points of his hose hanging loose. These are what he uses to secure his hose to his doublet. Usually he wears a hat but he has discarded this also. He is holding his scythe, the handle of which has been carved from a naturally curved piece of willow, and by his side you can see a large earthenware jug which holds water for the labourers.

Adam is looking out for his wife, Joanna, who is is also working in the fields. She is going to join him and some of the other men and women for something to eat and drink.

Joanna is wearing a linen hood with the tails securely fastened out of the way. Her kirtle bodice is laced at the front and she has the sleeves of her chemise rolled up. She has her kirtle and apron hitched up to allow her more freedom of movement and, because of this, you can see her shoes. They are made of rushes. She is carrying her straw hat, a large jug and her rake.

Adam and Joanna are very poor and live in a tiny, one-roomed cottage. This time of year is very important to them for they can earn a little extra money. A good harvest will mean that it will be a little easier for them to survive the winter. At the end of the harvest, William and Alice will provide a harvest supper which will be attended by all the farm labourers. Adam and Joanna always look forward to this occasion of feasting and merriment.

A Herald and Peasants, c. 1534

This is Edmund, the nobleman's herald and the son of the merchant we met earlier. The distinctive feature of a herald's clothing was always his tabard. This consisted of two rectangular pieces of material which were joined over the shoulders and put on over the head. A small panel would normally overhang each shoulder like an open sleeve or half cape. Edmund's tabard is decorated with the nobleman's family crest. He is also wearing a short doublet, tight hose and soft leather boots with turn-over tops.

He is hurrying back to the castle with the exciting news that the King is soon to visit the nobleman during one of his royal progresses. This is a great honour for the nobleman, but it will be very costly because the King will be accompanied by a vast retinue who will all have to be housed, fed and entertained. There will be feasting, dancing and jousting tournaments which must be financed by the nobleman and organized by his servants.

On his journey Edmund passes Adam and Joanna who are dressed in their best clothes and are hurrying to their own celebrations — the harvest supper and dance. They are very excited by Edmund's news as it means that they will have the opportunity to see King Henry and his new queen, Anne Boleyn, as they ride through the countryside.

Even though they are feasting and merrymaking, the peasants' clothes are very simple, as you can see, with none of the slashing and ornamentation that the fashionable courtiers are wearing.

Henry VIII and Anne Boleyn, c. 1534

Here are Henry and Anne at the castle in all their splendour. Look carefully at the beauty of their clothes, which are slashed, embroidered and studded with jewels. Anne spent some time in France when she was young, as a lady-in-waiting to Henry's sister, Mary Tudor. She liked the French fashions and here she is seen wearing a French hood which is fashionable at Court and will, no doubt, be copied by the ladies of the nobleman's household after her visit!

Henry at the Tournament, c. 1534

Here you can see Henry on horseback, armed and ready for the tilt. He and his horse are protected by armour against the weapons of the opponent. It was the custom for the competitors in the tilt to display their family colours and coat of arms. Henry, therefore, is displaying the Tudor Rose. Can you identify it?

Jousting was a pastime enjoyed by many nobles and had been popular since mediaeval times. It could be dangerous, however, as the object of the game was to shatter the opponent's lance and throw him from his horse. Once, in 1524, Henry was trying out a new suit of armour at a jousting tournament and forgot to put down the visor on his helmet. The Duke of Suffolk, who was his opponent at the time, struck Henry a blow which nearly killed him. This demonstrates the importance of the protective clothing which they always wore. In fact, the King was destined to have another accident in 1536, which injured him and curtailed his sporting activities for good.

Jousting was always a good time for display, and sometimes the competitors wore grotesque masks like the one pictured below, which was given to Henry by the Emperor Charles V.

On the right you can see the nobleman dressed in his armour, ready for a jousting match with King Henry. The armour used in jousting would be the same as that worn on the battlefield.

Try to find out more about the customs involved in jousting and the type of weapons and armour used by those taking part.

grotesque mask

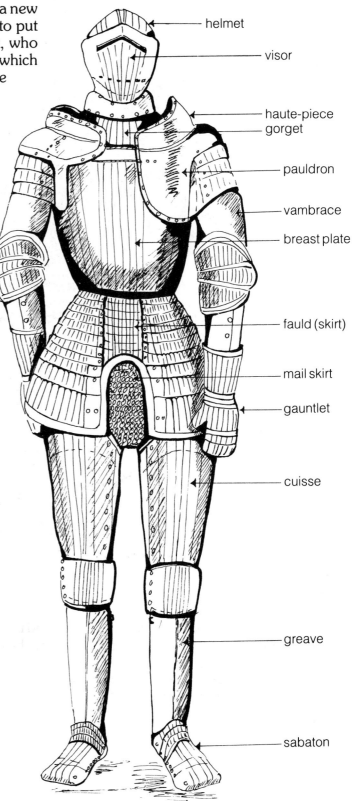

helmet

visor

haute-piece

gorget

pauldron

vambrace

breast plate

fauld (skirt)

mail skirt

gauntlet

cuisse

greave

sabaton

31

The King's Fool, c. 1534

Here are some of the people who will provide entertainment during the feasting and celebrations. This is Will Somers, the King's fool, or jester, who has been with King Henry for many years. Physically, he is the very opposite of Henry, being thin and stooping, with a slight hunchback. Even though Will comes from a very humble background, a great friendship exists between the two men and Will can say many things to the King that high Court officials would not dare. This is because Will has his fool's 'licence'. (You might like to think about this in connection with the saying: 'Many a true word is spoken in jest.') When you study Shakespeare's plays you will see that he often has a fool, like Will, who shows great wisdom through simple jesting.

Will's clothing is plain, consisting of a long, skirted doublet with a hood over a high-necked shirt, tight hose and soft leather shoes. He has a bag suspended from his belt. Usually when he is entertaining he carries a pet monkey with him and he often wears a more traditional jester's costume like that pictured opposite.

Life at King Henry's Court could be very precarious. Anyone who offended the King was dealt with harshly, sometimes even losing his or her life. Will Somers managed to remain a great favourite with King Henry for many years, however. What kind of jokes and tricks do you think he used to play in order to please his master and all the courtiers?

A jester, c. 1490

A bagpiper, c. 1520

A fashionable lady,
c. 1527

King Henry VIII,
c. 1539

A fashionable lady,
c. 1540

Sir Martin Frobisher and a young sailor, c. 1577

Sir Francis Drake,
c. 1588

Queen Elizabeth I,
c. 1592

A young man, c. 1595

Court Musicians, c. 1534

The Tudors were very fond of music and here are three Court musicians. Their garments are also very simple and a little old-fashioned. Their headwear, for example, would have been more fashionable in the 1490s than in 1534. They are playing the pipe and tabor, the harp and clavichord.

You might like to find out more about some of the unusual instruments that were popular at this time.

Two Travellers, c. 1534

While all this feasting and merrymaking is taking place, however, outside there are many others who have little cause for celebration.

This is a Benedictine monk. He is wearing a black habit of wool with wide sleeves, and he has a cowl pulled over the back of his head. His hair is tonsured, which means that the centre of his head is shaved. The three knots in his girdle symbolize his religious vows of poverty, chastity and obedience.

This monk is homeless because his monastery has been closed by Thomas Cromwell, the King's chief minister, and he is now journeying along the road seeking shelter. This is rather sad because for many years he has provided help, food and shelter for all the weary travellers and homeless peasants who came to him, like the young man on the opposite page, who has just passed the monk on the road.

This is Ned, who is a cousin of Will Somers. Ned used to work as a labourer on his father's farm but his family have now lost their farm and livelihood due to the enclosure of some common grazing land. Ned has travelled far in order to see his cousin and try to get help from him.

His clothes are old and ragged, consisting of thin, tattered hose, loose-fitting, square-toed leather boots and an old-fashioned tunic over a shirt. He carries a basket on his back in which there is a little food and a blanket.

Perhaps you would like to think about the different fortunes of Will Somers and his cousin Ned, who both came from the same background. Also, you might be interested to investigate some of the effects that the dissolution of the monasteries and the enclosure of common land had on the poor.

A Fashionable Lady, c. 1553

We are now going to move forward in time to the year 1553 and to the Court of Mary Tudor, who is now Queen of England following the death of the young King Edward.

This is Elizabeth, the nobleman's granddaughter who you saw as a baby in 1534. She is now a young lady at Court and is wearing the latest fashion.

Her gown has a well-fitting bodice with a low waist and a stiff collar edged with lace. The skirt spreads out stiffly from the hips to the hem and has an inverted V cut out at the front which is filled in with a forepart of rich material. The sleeves reach to the elbow, with undersleeves of contrasting material. The borders around the top of the armholes are called 'pickadils'.

She is wearing the English version of the French hood, which is flatter than the more curved French hood which you can see on the opposite page.

You will notice that in both pictures of Elizabeth her chemise has a high neck. This is a significant development as it marks the beginnings of the fashion for ruffs, which was so popular in later years.

Under her gown she is wearing a Spanish farthingale, which was an underpetticoat with a series of hoops, smaller at the top, inserted into it at intervals. The farthingale was, in fact, very similar to the crinoline which was fashionable in Queen Victoria's reign.

On this page you can also see some other items from Elizabeth's wardrobe. One interesting point to bear in mind is that although her clothes are very beautiful and ornate they would be stiff and heavy and probably most uncomfortable.

Can you think of any reasons why the English fashions were influenced by the Spanish fashions at this time?

jewelled pomander –
to counteract
unpleasant odours!

French hood, chain necklace

hairpin of
carved bone

wooden comb

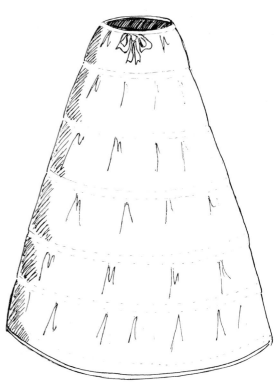

Spanish farthingale

A Scholar and Physician, c. 1553

This is Richard, Elizabeth's brother, who is also in London. He is a scholar and a physician. Richard is dressed in the fashions of the day, but he has two distinguishing features denoting his profession. These are his long gown and his headwear, which consists of a flat bonnet worn over a coif. The gown and the coif were usually worn by physicians as they gave them a diginified appearance.

You will notice, looking at Richard's clothes, that the fashions have not changed a great deal since the reign of Henry VIII except for a few minor points. This was partly because the young King Edward had not been old enough to take a great interest in clothes and, as we have seen, changes in fashion usually originated at Court.

Broad-toed shoes were being replaced by shoes with a more rounded or pointed toe and the codpiece, although being worn by Richard, was beginning to go out of fashion at this time. Necklines were becoming higher and waists a little more pointed at the front — you will see both these characteristics develop in a very exaggerated way during the reign of Elizabeth I.

Also pictured here are a few of Richard's accessories, along with his medicine chest and a few of his surgical instruments. Medicine was, of course, very primitive in 1553. Perhaps you could investigate some of the ways in which doctors like Richard tried to cope with the serious plague epidemics which occurred from time to time.

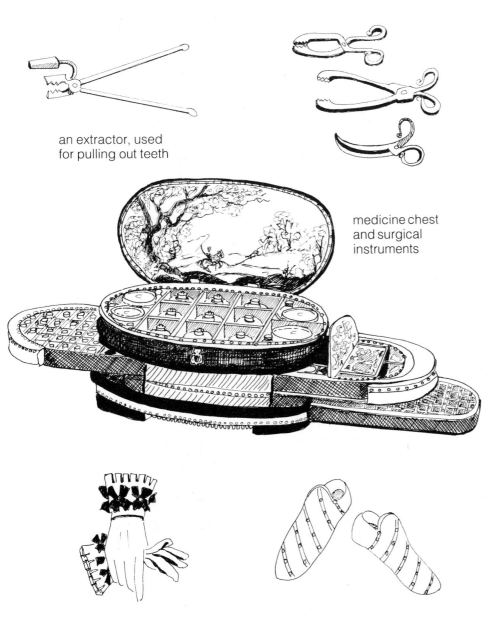

an extractor, used
for pulling out teeth

medicine chest
and surgical
instruments

gloves

leather shoes

leather bag

A Noblewoman, c. 1565

It is now 1565. Elizabeth has married a nobleman who is one of Queen Elizabeth's counsellors, and they live in a large manor house with their family. They are very wealthy and Elizabeth is usually dressed in the latest fashions.

Here she is wearing an elaborate gown with a low, square neck which has been filled in with a partlet with a standing collar. The sleeves are large and puffed at the shoulders and have tight-fitting undersleeves. The skirt is worn over a Spanish farthingale and has a forepart of contrasting material. She has a jewelled girdle and on her head a jewelled caul.

You will notice that she is carrying a handkerchief. The idea of holding a handkerchief for ornamental display rather than for use was new at this time, and it is an idea that has remained with us ever since.

You will see from the picture below that bonnets were also becoming fashionable and women often wore them in preference to the more cumbersome headdresses that you have seen before. Also pictured here are some of Elizabeth's accessories.

Even though the fabrics and decoration on ladies' dresses were so beautiful, hygiene and cleanliness still left a lot to be desired. This was an age before toothbrushes, and a toothpick was the principal means of cleaning the teeth. Wealthy people often used ornamental toothpicks like the one below.

In addition to pomanders and posies of flowers, many ladies tried to disguise bad smells in the home by burning herbs over charcoal in a small pottery stove.

bonnet with feather, small neck ruff

toothpick in gold and porcelain

fan

lute

herbal fumigator

leather shoe with cut-outs

shoe with high-cut sides

A Nobleman, c. 1565

This is Robert, Elizabeth's husband. He is wearing a sleeveless jerkin over his doublet and a small ruff. His bonnet has a jewelled hatband and a feather, and his shoes are bluntly pointed.

His trunk hose is interesting in that it is paned and bombasted. Panes were bands of cloth joined at the end so that they gaped when the wearer moved, giving a similar effect to slashing. Bombast was a padding material used inside the trunk hose and could be made of cotton or wool rags, flax, flock, horsehair or bran.

Padding of this kind meant that trunk hose began to assume gigantic proportions. Soldiers found them useful for storing loot and some wearers could not even sit comfortably on an ordinary chair! A special scaffold was erected in the Houses of Parliament for those who took up too much room with their padded breeches!

If you look at the picture on the left you will see just how much the shape of fashion has changed since the reign of Henry VIII. In Henry's time, the trend was a for a square, aggressive, masculine appearance, but in 1565 the fashion was to have a small waist and exaggerated hips, which was a more feminine look. One factor that might have contributed to this change was that there was now a woman on the throne, and a queen who was admired and respected as much as Henry VIII had been.

Elizabeth I once referred to herself as having the qualities of a man even though she had the appearance of a woman:

I have the body of a weak and feeble woman,
but I have the heart and stomach of a King . . .

How do you think all this relates to the changing shape of fashion?

pleated bonnet,
small ruff

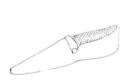

leather shoe

embroidered purse

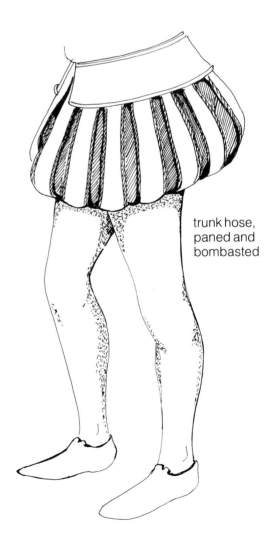

trunk hose,
paned and
bombasted

embroidered shirt

The Nobleman's Children, c. 1569

This is 14-year-old Cecily, the eldest daughter of Robert and Elizabeth. Her clothes are rich and beautiful as befit the daughter of a nobleman. On her head she is wearing a jewelled bonnet over a caul and more jewels and chains adorn her neck, hands and the bodice of her gown. Her gown is made of a rich velvet with contrasting sleeves, partlet and forepart. A white sash serves as a girdle and she has a ruff at her neck and at each sleeve.

Nicholas, her younger brother, is a page at the Court of Queen Elizabeth. He is dressed very finely in an outfit given to him by the Queen. He is wearing a close-fitting doublet that has been decorated with slashes and pearls, and his trunk hose are paned and bombasted. Around his waist, under his belt, you can see the points that join his trunk hose to his doublet. On his chest he is wearing a jewelled Tudor Rose, signifying that he is in the Queen's service.

Because Nicholas's clothes have been given to him as part of the job they do not belong to him but to the Crown. Therefore, if he were to leave his job he would have to return them, or else he would be branded a thief!

Little Catherine is five years old. She is wearing a gown with detachable, unmatching sleeves, an apron with a bib and a matching collar, known as a 'falling band'. On her head she is wearing a coif under a small Mary Stuart hood, made popular by – and named after – Mary Queen of Scots.

These children are dressed very finely in the fashions of their day, but think how stiff, uncomforable and unhealthy these clothes must have been! For example, it was the custom to corset little girls from a very early age, so Catherine is probably wearing a very tight corset under her garments in order to shape her figure for the future. What sort of effect do you think this would have on a five-year-old child?

A Tailor and His Family, c. 1569

This is a middle-class Tudor family. James, the father, is the grandson of the merchant whom you met earlier in the book (1534). James is now a prosperous tailor and lives with his family in London. Their clothes, therefore, are fashionable but not, of course, as extravagant as those of the nobleman's family.

Dorothy is at home with two of their children, Frances and baby Philip. She is wearing a cotton lawn cap and an embroidered gown with matching forepart and sleeves. Frances is wearing a long gown with winged sleeves and an apron. She is holding a rattle which is tipped with a stick of coral. You can see that baby Philip is tightly bandaged in his swaddling bands underneath the blanket that is around him.

James is in his shop, cutting material that has been imported from Italy. He is going to make it into a fine gown for the nobleman's wife, who visits his shop from time to time.

He is wearing a short doublet and padded trunk hose, with a small ruff at his neck and at each wrist. On the wall you can see his tailor's sign. A similar sign hangs outside his shop. Try to find out more about the middle classes in Tudor times and about the fortunes of men like James. Also, if you look at the colour section of this book, you will see what happened to baby Philip.

A Schoolboy, c. 1569

This is Luke, the tailor's eldest son, who is on his way to school. He is wearing a belted jerkin over his doublet and he has a small ruff at his neck and one at each sleeve. His trunk hose are paned and he has socks over his stockings. He is carrying his hat, and in his satchel he has his ink horn and bird's feather quill pen. He may also have a horn book like the one pictured below. This was a simple wooden frame with a single page mounted upon it which was then covered with a sheet of horn.

School life was hard in Elizabethan times. The day usually began at six or seven o'clock in the morning and went on until five o'clock at night. Many of the lessons would be Latin grammar, as Latin was taught as a living language. Often pupils were expected to speak in Latin, even during playtime. Other subjects taught included Religious Knowledge, Greek, Hebrew, Logic and Rhetoric (the art of public-speaking). Beatings from the schoolmaster were frequent as discipline was harsh.

On the opposite page you can see the schoolroom and the master dressed in his coif, cap and long gown. In his hand he is carrying a birch rod with which to beat the boys. No wonder Shakespeare wrote about the sixteenth-century schoolboy 'creeping like a snail unwillingly to school'!

horn book

bird's feather
quill pen

A Street Trader and Her Husband, c. 1570

In Elizabethan times the streets of London were alive with noisy, bustling crowds of people. Here are some of the characters that Luke might meet on his way home from school.

This is Martha. She and her husband sell eggs, bread and vegetables from a stall in the street. She is wearing a wide-brimmed, flat-crowned hat over a linen hood, and her coarse linen chemise is drawn into a ruffle around her neck. Her gown is laced at the bodice and has slashes at the sleeves. Martha does not have the money to buy fine fashionable clothes, so her garments seem plain compared to those worn by Elizabeth and Dorothy, but Martha's clothes are well suited to her lifestyle. Farthingales and ornaments would be out of place in the busy and filthy streets of London.

Her husband has gone to collect more vegetables for the stall. He is wearing a coarse linen tunic, thick hose and stockings, and tough leather boots. This outfit is very old-fashioned indeed, but once again, practical for his work. Bombasted and paned hose would only hamper his movements whilst he was carrying and lifting heavy baskets of fruit and vegetables.

He is also wearing a woollen cap. At about this time Queen Elizabeth issued a proclamation which decreed that everyone over six years of age, except nobility or other persons of rank, had to wear a knitted woollen cap on Sabbath days and holy days. This law was passed in order to protect the British wool trade which was suffering due to the increased use of imported silks and velvets from the Continent. The woollen cap became known as the 'statute cap', but the law was quite difficult to enforce and had to be repealed in 1597.

How do you think people would react today if there were a law passed making it compulsory to wear certain garments?

Two Wanderers, c. 1570

This is Gilbert, the farmer's son whom you met earlier in the book. He joined a company of travelling actors when they were touring near his home in the Midlands and now Gilbert is performing in London with them.

He is wearing a felt hat with an ostrich plume, a fitted doublet with a short skirt, paned hose and leather boots. He is standing on a wooden platform which serves as a stage. Gilbert usually wears his own clothes for a performance. Sometimes the actors make use of masks and props and the boy members of the company dress as women when playing female parts.

The life of a travelling actor was not an easy one, and companies had to rely on sponsorship from rich men like the nobleman.

Try to find out more about travelling actors in Elizabethan times.

Wandering pedlars and hawkers were a familiar sight in Tudor times. This pedlar has spent most of his life wandering the streets of London and the nearby villages selling his wares.

His clothing is old-fashioned but, nevertheless, he makes a colourful figure in his wide-brimmed hat, shabby belted tunic, thick hose and leather shoes. He has a bag suspended from his belt and pieces of linen tied around his calves. In his tray he has pomanders, mirrors, gloves, cards, notebooks and other trinkets for his customers.

A Fashionable Lady, c. 1580

We have now moved on 15 years to 1580. Here is Catherine, the little girl you saw earlier, who is now 21 years old. Because she comes from a wealthy family her clothes are always fashionable.

Her gown has a V-opening to the waist, filled in with a stomacher, the material of which matches the inverted V-opening of the skirt. Above the stomacher you can see her chemise, which is gathered up to her neck under the ruff. The gown has hanging sleeves, which have been copied from male fashions and which have become very popular, and a high collar with a wired support. Her hair is swept up from her face and secured under a lace cap.

You will notice that the ruff has now become exaggerated.

In 1564 starch was introduced into England by a Dutch lady. The demand for education in starching was so great that the enterprising woman started giving expensive lessons on 'how to starch' to wealthy ladies. This meant that as knowledge of starching gradually became more widespread the ruff began to grow enormously and was very popular with both sexes.

Can you imagine how uncomfortable Catherine's clothes must be? When you remember that she is tightly corsetted, is wearing a farthingale, a starched ruff, a wired collar, a stomacher stiffened with pasteboard and several layers of heavy material, it is difficult to believe that she can even walk!

Also pictured here are some other items from her wardrobe. The 'taffeta pipkin' was a popular style of bonnet that was usually worn over a hair net or caul.

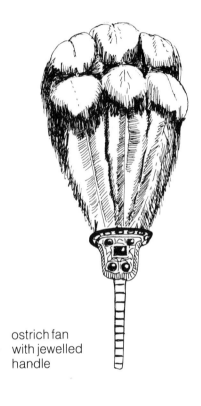

ostrich fan
with jewelled
handle

'taffeta pipkin'

square-toed shoe
with ribbon rosette

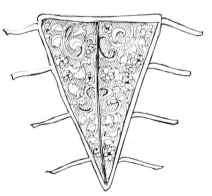

embroidered
stomacher

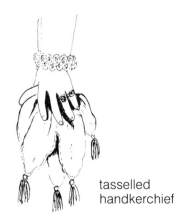

tasselled
handkerchief

A Fashionable Gentleman, c. 1580

Here is Catherine's brother Nicholas, whom you last saw dressed in his page's outfit. He is now a grown man and a firm favourite with Queen Elizabeth at Court. Here you can see him dressed in the lastest fashions.

His doublet is interesting because it has a 'peascod' belly. This was a very strange fashion that involved padding the front of the doublet so that it overhung the waist like a paunch. The padding had a pointed shape and sometimes was as much as nine inches long, so that it was almost impossible for the wearer to bend over.

This must be one of the few occasions in history when man has exaggerated his stomach instead of concealing it, and it is interesting that Punch, from Punch and Judy, is still portrayed with a peascod belly even today.

Nicholas is also wearing 'canions'. These are an extension of his short trunk hose and end just above his knees. Sometimes he might wear Venetian hose, like those pictured on the opposite page. These could be pear-shaped and baggy, or quite close-fitting.

His shoes are made of leather and have long tongues. Over these he wears a pair of 'pantoffles', a kind of overshoe, which would be very useful in the filthy London streets.

He is carrying his Court bonnet, though he might easily wear a different style of hat, like the one picture below.

As you can see, Nicholas's clothes look almost as uncomfortable as his sister's, with all the padding and the large, starched ruff. One writer in Elizabethan times complained that ruffs were becoming so large that they were 'abominable and detestable' and 'the Devil himself would be ashamed to wear one'!

In the colour section of the book, you can see two famous men who were involved in the Spanish Armada in 1588. If you look at their clothes you will see that they are very similar in style to those pictured here.

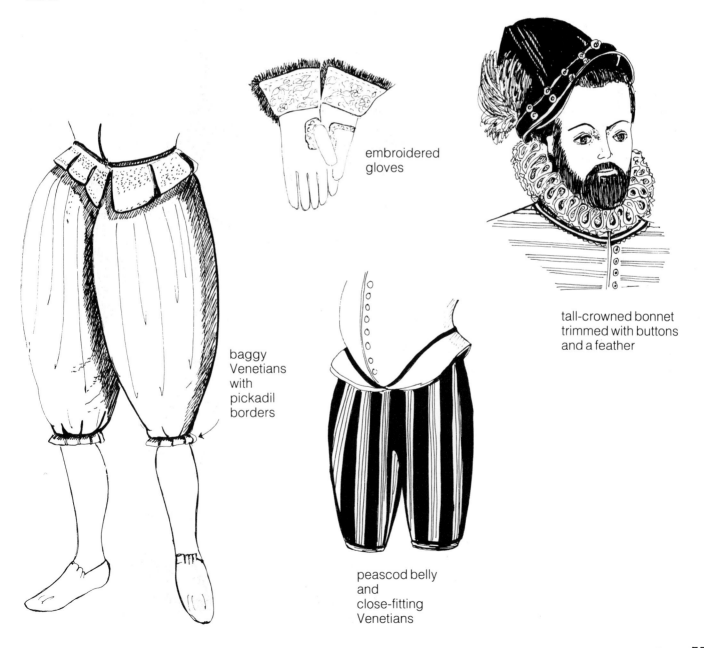

embroidered
gloves

baggy
Venetians
with
pickadil
borders

peascod belly
and
close-fitting
Venetians

tall-crowned bonnet
trimmed with buttons
and a feather

The French Farthingale, c. 1590

It is now 1590 and here is Catherine, once again in the latest fashions. Her maid is helping her to dress and is tying on a French farthingale.

There were two types of French farthingale which were popular at this time. The first was the padded roll or 'bum roll', which was inserted under the gown to make it stand out at the hips. The second was the wheel farthingale, a wheel-shaped structure made of wire or whalebone and worn around the waist. (You can see Queen Elizabeth wearing one of these in the colour section of the book.)

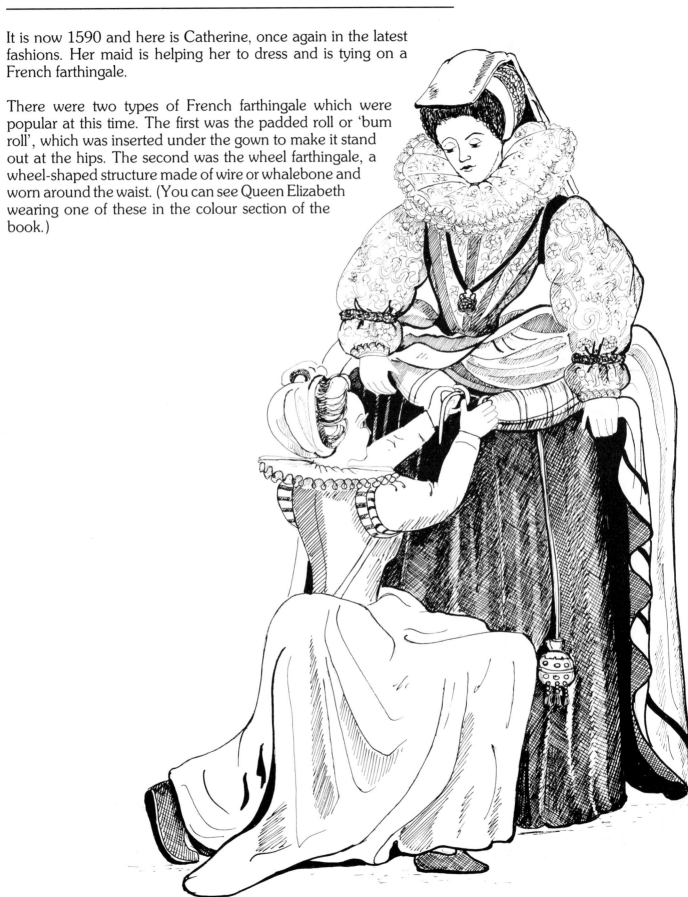

This seems to us today yet another strange and cumbersome fashion. It was occasionally also quite impractical, for some ladies wearing wide wheel farthingales were unable to walk through narrow doorways!

Catherine's maid, Frances, the tailor's daughter, is very plainly dressed compared to her mistress. She is not wearing a farthingale at all, because it would hamper her movements. Her hair is simply secured in a plain linen hood, the ends of which have been tied over her head. This also is in contrast to Catherine's fine 'bongrace' headdress, which she is wearing over a caul.

These two ladies provide an interesting contrast in appearance. One is stiff, starched, jewelled and padded, and the other is softer, simpler and more practical. Which do you think you would have preferred to wear?

embroidered
coif, c. 1586

the French
wheel farthingale

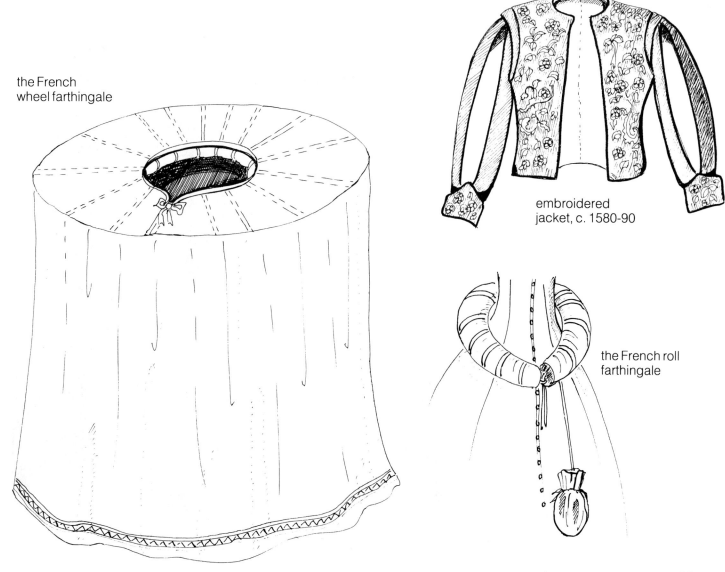

embroidered
jacket, c. 1580-90

the French roll
farthingale

Conclusion

As we leave the Elizabethans struggling into their starched ruffs, tight corsets and padded skirts and breeches, you might like to reflect on how much the shape of fashion changed during the sixteenth century. Women's clothes moved from simple, flowing lines to rigid and more angular shapes, while men's clothes changed from being aggressively masculine, with broad, padded shoulders, to a more feminine look, with small waists and padded hips. Can you think of any reasons why these changes might have occurred?

It is also worth remembering how uncomfortable these clothes must have been, even though they looked so splendid. You could try constructing an Elizabethan ruff or a cartwheel farthingale for yourself and then imagine what it would be like to wear these garments all day long. Why do you think men and women went to such lengths to disguise their natural shape with so much padding and wiring?

When studying costume, it is always interesting to note how often fashions turn up again in the future. The Spanish farthingale, for example, is very similar to the Victorian crinoline. Perhaps you will come across other examples like this in your work. Some items of Tudor costume remain with us even today: the gable headdresses of the Tudor ladies and the jester's costume appear on our playing cards, and the peascod belly of the Elizabethan men has survived in the character of Punch. Can you think why these particular traditions should have survived?

60

Finally, we must remember that these changing fashions were worn only by those who could afford them and that the garments of many town and country folk changed very little throughout our period. Also, as we have seen, starching, padding, ruffs and farthingales would have been impractical for those trying to work, even if they had been able to afford fashionable clothes.

Using some of the ideas in this book, you might like to investigate the very varied types of clothing worn by people in Tudor society and think how there were adapted to suit different ways of life. Is there still a distinction between fashion and costume? How are our clothes today suited to the kinds of jobs we do?

Glossary

aiglets	decorative metal tags on the ends of points *(page 9)*
biggin	a baby's cap *(page 17)*
bombast	padding material which could be made of cotton or wool rags, flax, flock, horsehair or bran *(pages 42, 45 and 47)*
bongrace headdress	oblong in shape and worn flat on the head, with one end forming a straight brim over the forehead to protect a woman's complexion from the sun *(page 59)*
canions	close-fitting extensions of the short trunk hose *(page 56)*
caul	a net or netted cap *(pages 40, 44, 55 and 59)*
codpiece	a bag covering the fork of the hose; sometimes used to contain money or a handkerchief *(page 8)*
coif	a close-fitting linen cap, tied under the chin *(pages 17, 38 and 49)*
cowl	a monk's hooded garment *(page 34)*
doublet	a close-fitting body garment worn by men *(page 9)*
farthingale	the Spanish farthingale was a skirt with a framework of wooden, circular hoops inserted into it. The French farthingale was of two types: the padded roll, worn around the waist, which gave fullness to the dress at the hips, and the wheel farthingale, which was a wheel-shaped structure made of wire or whalebone and worn around the waist *(pages 37, 58 and 59)*
falling band	a soft, unstiffened collar *(page 45)*
forepart	the exposed part of an underskirt when there was an inverted V-shape cut into the front of a lady's skirt *(pages 36, 40 and 44)*
French hood	a hood worn in England from about 1530-90. It was based on a stiff metal frame and set back on the head to display the hair in front. A velvet curtain hung down the back of the neck in folds *(pages 29, 36 and 37)*
gable hood	another name for an English hood. The front was shaped like a gable *(page 11)*
hose	leg coverings, rather like our 'tights'. These could be divided into two distinct parts: the breeches, or upper stocks and the lower half or nether stocks *(pages 8 and 13)*
kirtle	an undergown worn by ladies *(pages 11 and 14)*
Mary Stuart hood	a style of cap with a wired edge dipping in the front and made popular by Mary Queen of Scots *(page 45)*
panes	bands of cloth sewn together at the end and used to decorate trunk hose or sleeves *(page 42)*
pantoffles	overshoes used to protect the footwear *(page 56)*
partlet	a separate fill-in for covering the neck and chest and worn with gowns with low necklines *(page 18)*
peascod belly	an unusual fashion, where doublets were padded in the front to overhang the belt like a paunch *(page 56)*
pickadil	a stiffened, tabbed or scalloped edge to finish off an armhole or waistband and add decoration *(page 36)*
points	laces used to fasten one garment to another *(pages 9 and 24)*
statue cap	a cap made of knitted wool, so called because in 1571 an Act of Parliament was passed making it compulsory for everyone over the age of six, except the nobility, to wear such a cap on Sabbath days and holy days *(page 51)*
slashing	cutting slits of varying lengths into a garment for decoration *(pages 8, 12, 13, 15, 28 and 29)*
stomacher	an ornamental panel made of rich and embroidered material and inserted into the front of a doublet or gown *(page 55)*
swaddling	the custom of bandaging a tiny baby from head to toe in order to protect it and to enable it to grow straight *(pages 16 and 46)*
tabard	a simple garment consisting of two rectangular pieces of material which were joined at the shoulders and put on over the head *(page 26)*
tonsure	the bare, shaven part of a monk or priest's head *(page 34)*
Venetians	knee-breeches fashionable for men. These could be baggy or close-fitting *(page 56)*

Book List

Ashelford, Jane	*A Visual History of Costume in the 16th Century*, Batsford, 1983
Black, J. A. & Garland, M.	*A History of Fashion*, 2nd ed. Orbis Publishing, 1980
Bradfield, Nancy	*Historical Costumes of England*, 2nd ed. Harrap, 1958
Brooke, Iris	*English Costume in the Age of Elizabeth*, Black, 1938
Contini, Mila	*Fashion from Ancient Egypt to the Present Day*, Hamlyn, 1965
Cunnington, C.W. & P.	*Handbook of English Costume in the 16th Century*, Faber, 1970
Cunnington, C.W. & P.	*The History of Underclothes,* revised ed. Faber, 1981
Cunnington, C.W. & Lucas, C.	*Occupational Costume in England*, Black, 1967
Cunnington, Phillis	*Costume of Household Servants from the Middle Ages to 1900*, Black 1974
Ganz, Paul (ed.)	*The Paintings of Hans Holbein*, Phaidon Press, 1956
Hansen, H.H.	*Costume Cavalcade*, Methuen, 1972
Kay, Marguerite	*Bruegel*, Hamlyn, 1969
Keyes, Jean	*A History of Women's Hairstyles 1500-1965*, Methuen 1967
Laver, James	*Costume*, Cassell, 1963
Laver, James	*Costume and Fashion, a Concise History*, 2nd ed. Thames and Hudson, 1982
Lister, Margot	*Costume, An Illustrated Survey*, Herbert Jenkins, 1968
Lofts, Norah	*Anne Boleyn*, Orbis Publishing, 1979
Mayo, Janet	*A History of Ecclesiastical Dress*, Batsford, 1984
Parker, K.T. (ed.)	*Selected Drawings from the Collection at Windsor Castle*, Phaidon Press, 1954
Plowden, Alison	*Elizabethan England*, Reader's Digest, 1982
Rupp, Gordon	*Thomas Moore*, Collins, 1978
Marion, Sichel	*Costume Reference, Volume 2: Tudors and Elizabethans*, Batsford, 1977
Squire, Geoffrey	*Dress, Art and Society 1560-1970*, Studio Vista, 1974
Stubbes, Phillip	*Anatomy of Abuses in England, 1583,* Truber & Co., 1877-9
Williams, Neville	*Henry VIII and His Court*, Weidenfeld & Nicholson, 1971
Williams-Mitchell, Christobel	*Dressed for the Job – the Story of Occupational Costume*, Blandford Press, 1982
Wilson, Derek	*England in the Age of Thomas Moore*, Granada, 1978
Wilson, Eunice	*A History of Shoe Fashion*, Pitman, 1974
Wright, L.B.	*Shakespeare's England*, Cassell, 1964
Yarwood, Doreen	*English Costume from the 2nd century B.C. to the Present Day*, Batsford, 1979

Places to Visit

There is, of course, very little surviving Tudor costume for you to look at in museums. However, it is helpful to look at paintings in art galleries, and here are a few ideas for some interesting places to visit:

Bath Museum of Costume, Assembly Rooms, Bath, Avon.

Geffrye Museum, Kingsland Road, Shoreditch, London E2 8EA.

The Mary Rose Exhibition, Portsmouth, Hants.

The National Portrait Gallery, St Martin's Place, Trafalgar Square, London WC2H 0HE.

The World of Shakespeare, Waterside, Stratford-upon-Avon, Warwickshire CV37 6DX.

Things to Do

1. Try making a cartwheel ruff out of paper or stiff material. How do you think it would feel to have to wear one of these all day?

2. Find out more about the wives of Henry VIII. Draw pictures of them and compare their clothes. How much did each of them influence fashion?

3. Find out more about jousting. With your friends, make a large drawing of a jousting tournament with the knights making a rich and colourful display.

4. Look closely at some of the patterns on the fabrics of the costumes worn by the rich in this book. Using these ideas, make some fabric designs of your own suitable for a wealthy Tudor man and his wife.

5. It was a well-known fact that Elizabeth I dyed her hair. See if you can discover more about how ladies coloured their hair in Tudor times. What other kinds of make-up did they use?

6. Find out as much as you can about children's clothes in Tudor times. Using this book to help you, do some drawings of their costumes. Write about the harmful effects that some of the clothes – for example, swaddling bands – might have had.

7. The Tudors were used to large banquets and ate a great deal of food. See if you can find out what might have been on the menu for a banquet during Henry VIII's reign. Who might be at the banquet? Who would be the most fashionable? What kind of clothes would the cooks and servants be wearing?

8. The Tudors took a great pride in their navy. Find out all you can about what the sailors used to wear and the kind of lives they led aboard ship. Look at the life of Sir Francis Drake in more detail and discover what kind of treasures he brought home from his raiding expeditions.

9. With a group of your friends, try making up some Tudor costumes, then act out a short scene together using some of the characters from this book.